Design Your Morning Routine

Jump-Start Your Daily Writing Success

WORKBOOK

Author Success Foundations Series Book 2

by
Christopher di Armani

https://ChristopherDiArmani.net

ISBN-13: 978-1988938097

Editor: Nicolas Johnson

Published by

Botanie Valley Productions Inc.
PO Box 507
Lytton, BC V0K1Z0

https://BotanieValleyProductions.com
Sales@BotanieValleyProductions.com

Dedication

This book is dedicated to my sweet and loving wife Lynda.

Without her unwavering support of my need to write every day…

This book would not be possible.

Acknowledgments

Without the assistance of my editor, Nicolas Johnson, I can't imagine how this book would read. He tears my words apart from every conceivable angle, then offers thoughtful and constructive criticism on how best to fix the destruction at our feet. I thank God for Nicolas Johnson and his talents, daily.

#EditorsMatter

Feedback Loop

I also wish to express my heartfelt gratitude to the following individuals who took time from their own busy lives to critique this manuscript. Their willingness to assist a total stranger humbles me.

Kim Steadman (KimSteadman.com)
Sharilee Swaity (Facebook.com/Sharilee.Swaity)

Read the Book First

Unless you read Design Your Morning Routine - Jump-Start Your Writing Success, the second book in the Author Success Foundations series, this workbook is almost useless. Chapter 3 is essential for you to develop an effective morning routine.

If you have not done so yet, visit this link to purchase the book from your favorite online retailer of by clicking the link below.

https://ChristopherDiArmani.net/morning-routine

What Is Your Current Morning Routine?

Everyone has a morning routine, even if it's not organized or intentional. You wake up, you hop in the shower, and you brush your teeth. Maybe you do a few other things as well. In the space below, make a list of everything you do from the moment you wake up until you leave for work.

The Morning Routine Test

The Morning Routine Test is a series of questions designed to show you how effective your current morning routine is at laying the foundation for a productive day.

1. Do you write every day?

❑	Yes, I write every day	10 Points
❑	No, I write 6 days per week. I take one day off	10 Points
❑	No, I take two days off every week	8 Points
❑	No, I only write 3 or 4 days per week	5 Points
❑	No, I write less than 3 days per week	0 Points

2. How much time do you set aside for writing each day?

❑	120 minutes or more	10 Points
❑	90 minutes or more	8 Points
❑	60 minutes or more	5 Points
❑	30 minutes or more	5 Points
❑	I don't write every day	0 Points

3. Before you go to sleep at night, do you select your wardrobe for the following day?

❑	Yes, every night	10 Points
❑	Yes, most nights	8 Points
❑	No, not consistently	4 Points
❑	No	0 Points

4. Before you go to sleep at night, do you make a list of your three most important tasks for the following day?

❑	Yes, every night	10 Points
❑	Yes, most nights	8 Points
❑	No, not consistently	4 Points
❑	No	0 Points

5. What time do you wake up?

❑	6am or earlier	10 Points
❑	6am - 7am	9 Points
❑	7am - 8am	8 Points
❑	8am - 9am	6 Points
❑	Whenever I feel like it	0 Points

6. How many hours do you sleep per night, on average?

❑	8 hours or more	10 Points
❑	7 hours - 8 hour	7 Points
❑	6 hours - 7 hours	3 Points
❑	Less than 6 hours	0 Points

7. Where is your phone when you go to bed at night?

❑	In another room of the house	10 Points
❑	Turned off	10 Points
❑	It's my alarm clock, but I set it on Airplane Mode	10 Points
❑	It's my alarm clock	3 Points
❑	In my bedroom but across the room	2 Points
❑	Beside my bed	0 Points

8. How many hours do you sleep per night, on average?

❑	8 hours or more	10 Points
❑	7 - 8 hours	8 Points
❑	6 - 7 hours	5 Points
❑	Less than 6 hours	0 Points

9. How do you wake up each morning?

❑	Naturally, when the sun wakes me up	10 Points
❑	With an alarm clock using a gentle sound	8 Points
❑	With an alarm clock using an annoying beep	3 Points
❑	With the radio tuned to the morning news	2 Points
❑	Whenever I wake up is when I wake up	0 Points

10. Do you hit the snooze button?

❑	No, I get out of bed as soon as my alarm goes off	10 Points
❑	No, but I don't get out of bed right away either	5 Points
❑	Yes, most days	2 Points

11. Do you drink coffee or tea in the morning?

❑	No, I don't need coffee or tea to wake up	10 Points
❑	Yes, I drink one cup (black) in the morning	8 Points
❑	Yes, I drink one cup with cream and/or sugar in the morning	7 Points
❑	Yes, I drink two cups (black) in the morning	6 Points
❑	Yes, I drink three or more cups in the morning	0 Points

12. Do you watch the morning television news?

❑	No	10 Points
❑	Yes, I need to know what's happening in the world	0 Points

13. Do you read the newspaper (physical or digital) or other online news site in the morning?

❑	No	10 Points
❑	Yes, I need to know what's happening in the world	0 Points

14. Do you listen to the radio in the morning?

❑	No	10 Points
❑	Yes, I need to know what's happening in the world	0 Points

15. Do you log on to social media in the morning?

❑	No	10 Points
❑	Yes, I log on to email, Facebook and/or Twitter for 30 minutes or less	3 Points

- ❑ Yes, I log on to Facebook and/or Twitter for more than 30 minutes — 2 Points
- ❑ Yes, I'm on social media pretty much from the time I wake up — 0 Points

16. Do you shower in the morning or at night before you go to bed?
    - ❑ Yes — 10 Points
    - ❑ No — 5 Points

17. If you shower, how long does it take you?
    - ❑ 10 minutes or less — 10 Points
    - ❑ 15 minutes — 5 Points
    - ❑ Longer than 15 minutes. Waking up is hard — 2 Points

18. Do you brush and floss your teeth in the morning?
    - ❑ Yes — 10 Points
    - ❑ Yes, both most days — 8 Points
    - ❑ Sometimes, but not consistently — 5 Points
    - ❑ No — 0 Points

19. If you brush and floss your teeth, how long does it normally take you?
    - ❑ Minimum of 2 minutes but less than 5 minutes — 10 Points
    - ❑ Longer than 5 minutes — 7 Points

20. Do you eat breakfast, or is coffee your breakfast?
    - ❑ Yes, I eat breakfast — 10 Points
    - ❑ No, I can't face food before 10am — 0 Points

21. If you eat breakfast, what do you eat?
    - ❑ A protein shake or smoothie — 10 Points
    - ❑ A selection of fresh fruit — 10 Points
    - ❑ Oatmeal — 10 Points
    - ❑ Yogurt (with or without fruit) — 10 Points
    - ❑ Bacon/sausages & eggs — 10 Points
    - ❑ Toast (with anything on it) — 5 Points
    - ❑ Anything else — 2 Points

22. Do you exercise in the morning (6 days per week)?
    - ❑ Every morning for at least 30 minutes — 20 Points
    - ❑ Every morning, for at least 15 minutes — 15 Points
    - ❑ Every morning, for 10 minutes — 10 Points
    - ❑ 3-4 times per week — 5 Point
    - ❑ Are you kidding? I'm lucky if I wake up in time to leave for work! — 0 Points

23. Do you drink a 16oz glass of water in the morning after you wake up?
    - ❑ Yes, every day — 20 Points
    - ❑ Yes, but not every day — 10 Points
    - ❑ Coffee has water. Does that count? — 0 Points

24. Do you spend any quiet time in meditation or daily devotions in the morning?
    - ❑ Yes, every morning for 15 minutes — 20 Points
    - ❑ Yes, every morning for 10 minutes or less — 10 Points

- ❑ Yes, but not on a regular basis — 5 Points
- ❑ What are meditation and daily devotions? — 0 Points

25. Do you create and go over a gratitude list in the morning?
    - ❑ Yes, every day — 20 Points
    - ❑ No, but I spend time thinking about what I'm grateful for each day — 15 Points
    - ❑ Yes, sometimes, but not every day — 10 Points
    - ❑ No — 0 Points
26. Do you make a list of priorities for the day ahead or review the list you made the night before?
    - ❑ Yes, every morning — 10 Points
    - ❑ Yes, sometimes — 5 Points
    - ❑ No, it's a total waste of time — 0 Points
27. Do you do anything to prepare for the following day before you go to bed at night?
    - ❑ Yes, every night — 10 Points
    - ❑ Yes, but not every night — 6 Points
    - ❑ No. Who has time? — 0 Points

How Did Your Score?

Your score: __________

If you score between 0 and 105 your morning routine is on critical life support.

If you score between 106 and 155 your morning routine has a few positive aspects but still needs serious assistance.

If you score between 156 and 205 you're doing okay, but there is much room for improvement.

If you score between 206 and 310 you're doing great. See if there is any part of your morning routine you can tweak to raise your score even higher.

While this test is not scientific in any way, it is based upon research of what helps make an individual more productive throughout their day.

First Things First

Now the fun begins. It's time to design your new morning routine. Your score in the Morning Routine Test, combined with the list of activities you perform after you wake up each day, gives you the necessary foundation to build your new routine.

1. Write down every task you do now, from the time you wake up until you leave for work.
2. If you did not do so in Chapter 2, take the Morning Routine Test now. Write down your score.
3. Examine your current morning routine. Cross off one item from your list you know is detrimental to your positive mindset.
4. Examine the list of 28 Morning Habits of Highly Successful People. Select one action to incorporate into your new morning routine to replace the one you deleted.
5. Beside each item on your list, write down how long you take to complete it.

For example, list brushing your teeth and taking a shower separately, and assign a time estimate to both. Repeat this process for every item on your list.

A healthy dose of patience serves you well throughout this process. New habits take time to build. Start small and build on your successes. This ensures you remain in a calm and positive mindset - an essential component of any good morning routine. You want to remove any possibility for a sense of failure to infiltrate your mind.

Your routine is not etched in stone. You can, and should, make changes as you are able. Don't push yourself. Remember, it takes two months for most people to build a new habit so it becomes automatic.

Every day, note how long you take to complete each part of your new morning routine. Record those times beside each item. At the end of each week, compare your estimated times with your actual times. Make any adjustments required.

The key, at this point, is flexibility. Since it takes 66 days, on average, to build a new habit, perform the same task every day for at least two months before you evaluating whether the habit works for you or not. If it helps you be more productive, is it automatic and routine, or do you need more practice until it becomes second-nature?

New York wasn't built in a day. New and beneficial habits aren't built overnight either. Be kind to yourself as you build this new routine into a habit.

I found it difficult to stay focused, initially. Then, about a month into my new routine I discovered I got angry when it was interrupted. I took this as a great sign. It meant the new routine was important to me - important enough to get angry when I was interrupted.

It also meant I took this new way of life seriously. This pleased me greatly.

If an addition to your routine doesn't work for you, replace it with something else you think might work better. Remember. It's your life. Mold this system so it works for you. The point is to improve your mindset and focus so you accomplish more every day.

Fill any empty blocks of time with a task from the list of 28 Morning Habits of Highly Successful People found in Chapter 3 of Design Your Morning Routine - Jump-Start Your Writing Success.

See how it goes for two months, until it becomes a habit. Adjust again, as needed. In two months time, evaluate how you feel at the start of your workday compared with how you felt before you started this program.

Write and tell me about it. I want to hear your story.

https://ChristopherDiArmani.net/contact/

Design Your Ideal Morning Routine

The list of 28 morning habits of highly successful people, found in Chapter 3 of "Design Your Morning Routine - Jump-Start Your Daily Writing Success," are suggestions, not Commandments. The list is gleaned from the morning routines of the world's most successful business men and women. These highly productive individuals credit their achievements to starting their day off right, with a pre-planned system in place to start their days.

In the space below, write down all the things from that list you would like to incorporate into your new morning routine.

This is NOT your new morning routine. This is the list of things you would like to incorporate into your morning routine if you had no limits on your time, energy or motivation.

Morning Routine Planner

Use this page to make changes to your morning routine. As you work through your morning routine, note how long it takes you to complete each individual task. For the first week, record those times beside each item. At the end of the week, if your estimated time differs vastly from your actual time, make the adjustment and carry on.

Morning Routine Planner

Use this page to make changes to your morning routine. As you work through your morning routine, note how long it takes you to complete each individual task. For the first week, record those times beside each item. At the end of the week, if your estimated time differs vastly from your actual time, make the adjustment and carry on.

Morning Routine Planner

Use this page to make changes to your morning routine. As you work through your morning routine, note how long it takes you to complete each individual task. For the first week, record those times beside each item. At the end of the week, if your estimated time differs vastly from your actual time, make the adjustment and carry on.

Morning Routine Planner

Use this page to make changes to your morning routine. As you work through your morning routine, note how long it takes you to complete each individual task. For the first week, record those times beside each item. At the end of the week, if your estimated time differs vastly from your actual time, make the adjustment and carry on.

Morning Routine Planner

Use this page to make changes to your morning routine. As you work through your morning routine, note how long it takes you to complete each individual task. For the first week, record those times beside each item. At the end of the week, if your estimated time differs vastly from your actual time, make the adjustment and carry on.

Morning Routine Planner

Use this page to make changes to your morning routine. As you work through your morning routine, note how long it takes you to complete each individual task. For the first week, record those times beside each item. At the end of the week, if your estimated time differs vastly from your actual time, make the adjustment and carry on.

Morning Routine Planner

Use this page to make changes to your morning routine. As you work through your morning routine, note how long it takes you to complete each individual task. For the first week, record those times beside each item. At the end of the week, if your estimated time differs vastly from your actual time, make the adjustment and carry on.

Morning Routine Planner

Use this page to make changes to your morning routine. As you work through your morning routine, note how long it takes you to complete each individual task. For the first week, record those times beside each item. At the end of the week, if your estimated time differs vastly from your actual time, make the adjustment and carry on.

Morning Routine Planner

Use this page to make changes to your morning routine. As you work through your morning routine, note how long it takes you to complete each individual task. For the first week, record those times beside each item. At the end of the week, if your estimated time differs vastly from your actual time, make the adjustment and carry on.

Morning Routine Planner

Use this page to make changes to your morning routine. As you work through your morning routine, note how long it takes you to complete each individual task. For the first week, record those times beside each item. At the end of the week, if your estimated time differs vastly from your actual time, make the adjustment and carry on.

Morning Routine Planner

Use this page to make changes to your morning routine. As you work through your morning routine, note how long it takes you to complete each individual task. For the first week, record those times beside each item. At the end of the week, if your estimated time differs vastly from your actual time, make the adjustment and carry on.

Morning Routine Planner

Use this page to make changes to your morning routine. As you work through your morning routine, note how long it takes you to complete each individual task. For the first week, record those times beside each item. At the end of the week, if your estimated time differs vastly from your actual time, make the adjustment and carry on.

Morning Routine Planner

Use this page to make changes to your morning routine. As you work through your morning routine, note how long it takes you to complete each individual task. For the first week, record those times beside each item. At the end of the week, if your estimated time differs vastly from your actual time, make the adjustment and carry on.

Next Steps

Do you struggle to "find time to write?"

No writer on earth "finds" the time. Time is not a commodity you earn but a finite resource you spend. Once spent, time cannot be recovered, recycled or reused. It's gone.

The issue is not our "lack" of time. The issue is our lack of focus.

Follow One Course Until Successful.

It sounds so simple, doesn't it? It is simple, but simple, as I stress repeatedly, does not mean easy.

If your current path delivered the results you want, this book would not catch your eye. If doing what you've always done yielded success, you'd be writing your book right now instead of spending your precious time here, with me, in search of answers.

Read the third book in the Author Success Foundations series, Author Focus - Develop Your Author Vision Statement and Laser-Focus Your Writing Career to learn how to create your personal author vision statement and unlock the keys to your ideal future.

Available from your favorite online book retailers today.

For more information, visit:

https://ChristopherDiArmani.net/design-your-morning-routine

www.ingramcontent.com/pod-product-compliance
Lightning Source LLC
LaVergne TN
LVHW061205120826
845149LV00011B/1917

* 9 7 8 1 9 8 8 9 3 8 0 9 7 *